PIGEONS

Written and designed by The Green Neighbor

Introduction

According to Encyclopedia Britannica, there are 352 species of pigeons. The name of the species Columbidae and is made up of pigeons and doves. Originally Western Asia, North Africa and Europe, pigeons can be found living in cities around the world." This book is an exploration of the lives of everyday pigeons from the perspective of their natural habitat in the urban setting.

What Exactly Is A Pigeon?

1. Pigeons belong to the kingdom Animalia and phylum Chordata.
2. Pigeons are birds and come under class Aves.
3. Pigeons belong to the order Columbiformes.
4. The family of pigeons is Columbidae.
5. The genus name is Columba and the species name is Livia
6. Therefore, the scientific name of the pigeon is Columbia Livia
7. Pigeons are the most common type of bird that thrives in Human ecosystems.

What's in My Genealogy?

Most pigeons are found in forests in moist tropical and subtropical forests. They naturally thrive on sea-side cliff settings. These are the origins of the common pigeons. From the "rock pigeon" and the rock dove" they became more commonly known as pests. These pigeons appear grayish blue in color with black bars and or iridescent green, purple, and white feathers on their necks and backs.

Pigeons: An Urban Bird

A common sight in urban areas. However, their presence can lead to various pest issues, such as soiling from the waste, damage to buildings, and some health risks. To effectively manage pigeon infestations, it is important to understand their behavior and habitat preferences and implement suitable handling remedies.

Why Do Pigeons Act Like This?

Pigeons are known for their migratory patterns and tendencies. They prefer nesting and roosting in protected areas such as building ledges and bridges.

Environmental Factors

When it's time to rest, pigeons like to make their homes in safe and cozy spots, like on building ledges and bridges. It's like they're building their own pigeon hotels up high! Isn't that neat?

Pigeons Droppings and Germs

Pigeon bodily waste is called droppings. They are an important matter of safety whenever pigeons are nearby. Their droppings are like vinegar and can cause sickness, eat away paint and statues over time.

Pigeon Deterrence

Management in the urban landscape

There are physical deterrents to prevent pigeon infestations. Bird spikes and netting are effective in preventing pigeons from landing on ledges and rooftops.

Electric shock systems create discomfort without harming the birds. Other deterrents, such as scarecrows and reflective materials, confuse and discourage pigeons from roosting.

Time outs for Pigeons!

Pigeon Remedies

To make sure pigeons don't cause too much trouble, make sure they don't find too much food lying around. By keeping trash nice and secure, we're sending the pigeons a clear message: If we don't put out too much food for them, they might decide to go somewhere else for a snack. Think.

"No buffet here!"

Now, when pigeons want to build their nests or take a rest, we can make some changes to their favorite spots. This way, they might decide, "Hmm, maybe I'll find a cozier place to chill!"

Natural Pigeon Repellants

Pest control methods for a comprehensive pigeon solution...

Avian (bird) repellents and taste deterrents can be applied to targeted areas. Botanical retardants and scent-based repellents, such as those containing grape extract or citronella, can deter pigeons.

Managing the Urban Pigeon

Urban areas require smart plans that put different things in play. First, we need to understand how pigeons act and think. We can use tricks to stop them from staying where we don't want them by using special stuff to make pigeons stay away or asking experts for help.

PIGEON POTION

Special Potions

There are special mixtures that can help out, like magic potions for pigeons. And don't forget if things get tough, there are always pros who know what to do to help.

The Ultimate Goal is Pigeon Control

Everything applied helps human beings to make sure, pigeons don't cause big problems.

And What's Good for Humans and Pigeons?

Keeps both feeling good and provides harmony to our living environment!

Pigeons

Our Neighbors in the Urban Landscape

The End.

Author Bio

The Green Neighbor is Tina Johnson, an environmental justice and public health advocate and a lifelong resident of West Harlem, NYC. The Green Neighbor is committed to building sustainable communities through knowledge and action.

With her history of community engagement, health education, and environmental activism, her books aim to grow environmental understanding through accessible topics and practical activities. Each book encourages readers to explore everyday actions that support local environments and promote stewardship.

The Green Neighbor believes small steps can lead to healthier, happier lives and a healthier planet. Her goal is to spark curiosity and inspire sustainable change—one neighborhood, one garden, or one habit at a time.